37975495R00057

Printed in Great Britain
by Amazon